DOGS

MICHAELA MILLER

Contents

Wild Ones 2

The Dog for You 4

Where to Find Your Dog 6

Healthy Dogs and Puppies 8

Feeding Time .10

Home Sweet Home 12

Stepping Out .14

Keeping Clean .16

At the Veterinarian 18

No more puppies 20

A note from the ASPCA 22

More Books to Read 22

Glossary 23

Index 24

Heinemann Library
Chicago, Illinois

Wild Ones

Dogs can be as big as a Great Dane or as small as a chihuahua. But no matter how big or small, all dogs are related to wolves.

Great Dane

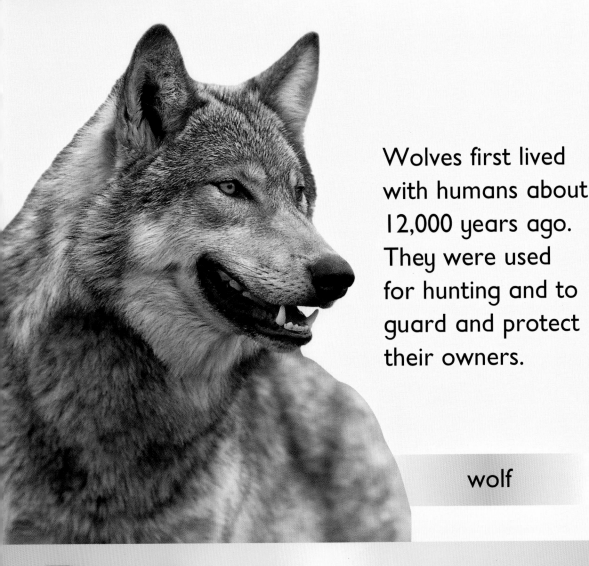

Wolves first lived with humans about 12,000 years ago. They were used for hunting and to guard and protect their owners.

wolf

Dogs can live for between ten and eighteen years. Smaller dogs usually live longer than large dogs.

3

The Dog for You

Dogs and puppies are lots of fun, but they also need a lot of looking after. If you and your family really want a dog, talk it over carefully.

DOG FACT

Around the world, more than 200 million dogs are kept as pets.

Ask a veterinarian for advice about the right type of dog for you. For example, some dogs are more active than others and need more space and exercise.

Where to Find Your Dog

Start looking for a dog at your local **animal shelter**. The people who work there should ask you all sorts of questions. They will also give you information on proper care.

dog at an animal shelter

Labrador puppies

If you want a special kind of puppy, a **pedigree** one, you need to get it from a **breeder**. This is a person who raises dogs. The veterinarian may know some good breeders.

Puppies should stay with their mothers until they are at least eight weeks old.

7

Healthy Dogs and Puppies

Healthy dogs and puppies have soft, clean, shiny coats and skin, without any lumps, cuts, or rashes. Their eyes are bright and clear. Their ears are soft and pink inside. They should have a moist, cold nose and a clean bottom.

a healthy dog

DOG FACT

Dogs need exercise and lots of company, otherwise they will be unhappy.

A happy dog or puppy will be happy to see you.

Feeding Time

Ask the veterinarian for advice about food. Big dogs need more food than small ones. Adult dogs need one or two meals a day. Puppies need three or four. Dogs and puppies must always have a bowl of fresh water.

You can buy dog food at supermarkets and pet supply stores. Follow the instructions carefully. Most dogs need a mixture of grains and meats.

DOG FACT

If you feed a dog or puppy too much, it will become fat and unhealthy.

Home Sweet Home

Dogs and puppies need a bed of their own. A chew-proof basket containing a washable mattress is a good idea. Some dogs like washable beanbags, too. Put the bed in a quiet place away from drafts.

DOG FACT

Dogs like toys, especially ones they can chew. Make sure the toys are strong, and not too small, or your dog might swallow them.

Your dog will need a brush and maybe a comb of its own. Ask the veterinarian which is the right kind for its coat.

Stepping Out

Dogs need to be walked two or three times a day and exercised at least once a day. Ask the veterinarian what sort of collar and leash you should buy. All collars should have **identification tags.**

All puppies and dogs need proper training. They must be trained to walk without pulling anyone over. They should come when they are called, sit when they are told, and stop when asked not to do something.

Dogs can carry diseases in their bodies. Always use a bag or pooper-scooper to clean up after your dog.

Keeping Clean

Make sure that your dog's food and water bowls are washed well after every meal. Its bed must also be kept clean.

a dog in a plastic basket

DOG FACT

When you brush your dog, you may find fleas. The veterinarian will tell you how to get rid of them.

Give your dog a bath when it is dirty. It will need to be brushed every day.

17

At the Veterinarian

Apart from you of course, the veterinarian is your dog's best friend. Take your dog for a checkup at least once a year. If your dog is sick, take it to the veterinarian immediately.

The veterinarian will give your puppy its first **vaccinations** when it is six to eight weeks old. After that the veterinarian will give your dog more **shots** when they are needed. These shots are very important. They could stop your dog from dying from some nasty diseases.

You should not walk a puppy on the street, or take it where other dogs have gone to the bathroom, until it has had all its shots, at about four months old.

19

No More Puppies

Puppies are very cute, but there are lots of them in the world and not enough people to look after them. You can stop your dog from making the problem worse by getting it **neutered**.

springer spaniel puppy

Dog Fact

Small dogs can have up to six puppies in one litter. Large dogs can have up to twelve.

collie puppies

Neutering is an operation which stops your dog from having puppies. It can also make your dog easier to live with and control. The veterinarian will tell you the best time for this operation to be done.

21

A Note From the ASPCA

Pets are often our good friends for the very best of reasons. They don't care how we look, how we dress, or who our friends are. They like us because we are nice to them and take care of them. That's what being friends is all about.

This book has given you information to help you know what your pet needs. Learn all you can from this book and others, and from people who know about animals, such as veterinarians and workers at animal shelters like the ASPCA. You will soon become your pet's most important friend.

MORE BOOKS TO READ

Fowler, Allan. *It Could Still be a Dog.* Chicago: Childrens Press, 1993.

Ring, Elizabeth. *Companion Dogs: More Than Best Friends.* Brookfield, Conn.: Millbrook, 1994.

Glossary

When words in this book are in bold, **like this**, they are explained in this glossary.

animal shelters There are many of these shelters all around the country that look after unwanted pets and try to find them new homes.

breeders People who raise and sell dogs and puppies are called breeders.

identification tag This is a small, flat disk of plastic or metal with your name, address, and telephone number on it. It may have your dog's name too. If your dog gets lost it can be used to make sure your pet is returned to you.

litter This is the name for a group of puppies born at the same time to the same mother.

neutering An operation to stop dogs from being able to have puppies is called neutering.

pedigree These are special dogs and puppies because we know their family history and how they should look.

shots Dogs have shots from a vet to stop them catching diseases.

vaccinations These are shots that protect your pet from diseases.

Index

brushing 13, 17

cleaning 16, 17

exercise 7, 14

feeding 10, 11

pedigree 7

sleeping 12

toys 13

training 14, 15

veterinarian 5, 10, 13, 14, 17, 18, 19, 21

wild dog 2, 3

wolves 2, 3

Published by Heinemann Interactive Library, an imprint of Reed Educational & Professional Publishing,
Chicago, IL
© 1998 RSPCA

Customer Service 1-888-454-2279
Visit or website at www.heinemannlibrary.com

Printed in Hong Kong / China
Designed by Nicki Wise and Lisa Nutt
Illustrations by Michael Strand

02 01
10 9 8 7 6 5 4

The Library of Congress has cataloged the hardcover version of this book as follows:

Library of Congress Cataloging-in-Publication Data
Miller, Michaela, 1961-
   Dogs / Michaela Miller.
      p. cm. — (Pets)
   Includes bibliographical reference and index.
   Summary: A simple introduction to choosing and caring for a dog.
   ISBN 1-57572-573-8 (lib. bdg.)
   1. Dogs — Juvenile literature. [1. Dogs. 2. Pets.] 1. Title.
   II. Series: Miller, Michaela. 1961- Pets.
   SF426.5.M565 1998   97-11983
   636.7'083—dc21   CIP
                            AC

Paperback ISBN 1-57572-478-2

Acknowledgments
The author and publishers are grateful to the following for permission to reproduce copyright photographs.
Dave Bradford pp4, 5, 8, 10-13, 16, 17; FLPA/p14 David Hosking; RSPCA/ pp2 John Howard, p3 Mark Hamlin, p6 Colin Seddon, p7 Steve Cobb, p15 Angela Hampton, pp18,19 Tim Sambrook, p20 E A Janes, p21 Dorothy Burrows; Tony Stone Images p9 Renee Lynn.
Cover photographs reproduced with permission of : RSPCA; Dave Bradford
With special thanks to the ASPCA and their consultant Dr. Stephen Zawistowski, who approved the contents of this book.
Every effort has been made to contact copyright holders of any material reproduced in this book.